Practical Local Business Marketing

Your guide to affordable local business marketing that works!

By

Lonnie Jay Rakestraw

Practical Local Business Marketing

First Printing, 2014

Printed in the United States of America

Published by SWR Publishing

Contents

Introduction

This book is the result of numerous consultations with local business owners. To say that most local business owners "don't know what they don't know" is an understatement. Business owners hear the buzzwords and they are slammed with sales calls all the time from companies trying to sell some sort of marketing service. But none of these people are helping to educate business owners, they just want to sell a service.

Perhaps the biggest problem for the business owner is that all these people are attempting to sell them a single piece of the puzzle (usually at a ridiculous price in my opinion). Until they sit down with me, most have never had someone take the time to explain the major tools that are available to them for their marketing efforts and how they fit together.

This book contains the same information that I have used successfully many times and now I am taking the time to share it with you. Written in a conversational tone, I want you to feel like you are getting advice from a friend. After reading this book, you will understand the key components of marketing a local business and how they fit together. Specifically, I want you to understand:

✓ What tools to use to get the greatest return on your investment.

✓ Why you want to use them.

✓ When it makes sense to use them.

✓ How to maximize their effectiveness.

This book does not contain a step-by-step guide to building a website. This is not a list of fifty tips that cover all areas of marketing where only a few are of any real benefit. You are not a "dummy" and don't need one of those guides.

Rather, this book is your guide to building a complete marketing strategy that is practical and doable. It is about understanding where your target market is looking for local products and services, how to reach them, and how to engage with them after you get them into your business so that you keep them.

Websites, engaging in social media, well targeted online ad campaigns, and many other such things are great tactical things that business owners can implement to help grow their business. But it is important to understand the big picture, how everything works together, so you will know when a specific tactic is appropriate and why you would want to use that tactic.

As an example, a website is the foundation of local marketing these days and will only grow in importance over time. Yet over half of all local businesses do not have one. Business owners that are serious about growing their business need to know why a website is a must-have investment and what makes for a great website. You can't just build a website and think that your marketing efforts are done. By the time you finish this book, you will know why that is the case.

Piece by piece, this book will walk you through a complete local marketing strategy that any business owner will be able to implement. I have set out to create a roadmap of how a business can become successful with their local marketing efforts - online marketing as well as a couple of the most successful offline methods that a business can use.

This book isn't going to show you step by step how to do every item that will be presented. That is not the purpose of the book. Local business owners need to understand the big picture before diving into the details. Also, facebook, Twitter, Google, etc. always have current guides available online. Any book with detailed instructions is obsolete as soon as one of the companies that provide the tools being used decides to change their interface. That happens very often in the online world. But the principles being covered have not changed for years.

This book will not contain any hype or grey areas. You will get a true picture of techniques that have been proven to work over the years and will continue to work for many more. You will be given techniques that are based on sound practices that I have spent years learning and using for my own clients. Through this book, you will learn just how simple building an online presence can be and you will learn the difference between what is necessary and what is hype.

While the process is simple, the time to implement the techniques outlined here are not inconsequential. Rarely will a business owner have the time or the inclination to do each of these steps themselves. For those that do, the steps are pretty intuitive and you can use the information in this book plus a little help from Google to find current in-depth "how to" information when you need some help.

My hope in writing this book is that business owners will be able to start seeing the "big picture" and thinking strategically about how they can leverage the (mostly) free tools available to them via Google and other online entities to capture their fair share of their local market.

This will be your strategic guide with tactical action items you can implement to help grow your business. But this needs to be approached as a process, not an event. Yes, it will take effort or a small marketing budget, but by using the principles in this book you will learn to quantify your marketing investment and measure the return on your investment (ROI). From there you will be able to make wise strategic investments that will pay themselves back many times over.

The layout of this book is a progressive step-by-step guide where each chapter builds upon the previous one. You will need to read every chapter, in the order presented, to get the full value from the information being provided. Skimming random chapters can give you some great information that can be used to help you grow your business, but taking the time to read each chapter and fully digest the information will pay dividends far greater than the sum of the parts.

Unfortunately, most of the books written for local business owners are written with the goal of selling them a website or other service. Not this one. While I do offer these same services when they will add value to a client's business, my core business is marketing consulting and helping small businesses define a strategy while getting the most for their money - not delivering the end product.

My clients are free to choose any company they want for fulfillment of the services I suggest. If you feel you need consulting after reading this book, I would love to hear from you. If you would like for my company to help with any area of implementation of any of the items we will cover, I would be happy to assist you with that as well. *But more than anything, I want to receive emails from local business owners who have taken the time to read and understand the principles outlined in this book and have applied them with success.*

This book will be written as clearly and free of industry jargon as possible. It will not have any theoretical or abstract concepts. There will be no talk of how easy it is to make millions with just a new website or how you can work four hours a week while travelling the globe and have money rolling into your bank account as if by some form of magic. This book will contain useful and practical information that any local business in any market can implement to grow their business.

It is also important to note that while the book is aimed at smaller local businesses, the principles here are largely applicable to any size business with an eye on any market. The difference is in the effort required in some of the tactical areas. If you are the owner of a larger business, this information, the "big picture" I keep referring to, is valuable to you as well.

Similarly, the information in this book is applicable for any local business in any country in the world. The list of citation sources in the chapter on building citations is for United States based local businesses, but the concepts are the same for any country in the world. Good practices are good practices everywhere!

Just one idea sparked by this book and put into action will be well worth the few dollars you are investing in this book as well as the couple of hours you invest to read and digest the information. You may even need to read it twice to let everything soak in. Your time invested in reading and applying the principles in this book is an investment in your business. If your business is important to you, make it a priority!

With that said, let's get started.

The role of marketing

According to Bloomberg, 8 out of 10 entrepreneurs who start businesses fail within the first 18 months. This is a staggering number and it makes one wonder why this is the case. Why are some businesses successful when their competition fails?

All things being equal, the business that does the best job of marketing their business will be the success story. The businesses that ignore a sound marketing strategy, do a poor job of identifying the opportunities available to their business, or a poor job of executing their marketing efforts will be counted among the failures.

Let's consider for a moment the case of two local barber shops in the same town competing for the same clients. Does barber A have some great technological advantage that barber B doesn't? No. Is barber A simply that much smarter than barber B? Probably not. Maybe barber A has mad skills that would make Edward Scissorhands envious. Well, I'm pretty sure that's not it. Some barbers are better than others, but is it to such a degree that everyone in town is amazed and other barbers are forced out of business? No.

So what is it that makes one business successful while another fails in the same environment with seemingly equal access to the same set of industry knowledge and similar technical skills? Not to discount the value of sound business practices, but substantially, it is about marketing.

One point that I always try to convey to business owners, and they usually look at me like I'm crazy, is that everyone is in the same business - selling. Your products and services may be different, one business sells flowers while another sells plumbing, but everyone is in the business of selling.

Often I hear from business owners that they "have the best prices" and "no one has the selection I have." While that may well be the case, does the best product always win in the marketplace? No. The product that is best marketed is usually the winner. In the early days of the PC, did Microsoft have the best operating system? Not even close. But Bill Gates did the best job of positioning and the rest is history.

That is why I wrote this book and titled it "Practical Local Business Marketing." The goal of this book is to help cut through all of the sales hype and false promises that run rampant in the marketing industry, especially in the area of internet marketing. The goal is to give business owners practical information on how they can lay a solid marketing foundation that is affordable, leveraging the free tools available on the internet, helping to drive more sales that lead to growth in their businesses.

If you want your business to be dominant, not just constantly in survival mode, strategic practical marketing is a must. And in order to focus on the most effective forms of marketing, you need to know your options. Likewise, you need to know how to calculate the effectiveness of your marketing efforts in order to know when it makes sense for YOUR company to engage in the various forms of marketing we will be covering in this book.

Before we begin, let's talk a little bit about customer care...

Getting a new customer in your doors is just the beginning

Most local business owners view getting a customer through their doors as the end goal of their marketing efforts. These business owners are making a huge mistake. Getting a new customer in your doors is just one step in the process. Repeat after me, "keeping my new customers is just as valuable as getting them in the first place." You can have the world's best marketing strategy and fail to maximize the potential of your marketing efforts due to poor customer service. If you want to be truly successful, it is imperative that all of your employees make a commitment to excellent customer care.

Word-of-mouth advertising always has been, and always will be, a fantastic method of getting new customers. When someone asks a friend or family member who they use for a product or service, that is the absolute best form of advertising that you can have - a recommendation from a trusted source.

Businesses that can deliver outstanding customer care will transform new first-time customers into loyal (valuable) REPEAT customers. Valuable repeat customers who are all over your city telling all of their friends and family members where to go to get your product or service. One new customer obtained through your marketing efforts could result in 10 customers easily through word-of-mouth advertising. The new customer tells a friend who tells a friend and on and on.

Businesses that fail to deliver quality products and services won't be getting these referrals and won't be in business very long. Businesses that don't deliver quality have walking billboards all over your city telling others where NOT to go! And the negative word-of-mouth advertising grows and grows. Don't let this happen to your business.

It may seem odd that a book on marketing your business starts out by talking about customer service but it seems that in this day and age that customer service has gone the way of the dinosaur. I recently went into a major department store and actually had to wait about five minutes for three associates to finish a conversation before I could get help from one of them.

Whether you are a dentist, chiropractor, a massage therapist, or any other provider of goods or services, your reputation matters. The one new client you get from the internet might tell ten of their friends and family members about their experience and you want that to be a good experience.

It has become cliché these days, but as we learned in Business 101 everything about a business comes down to people, processes, and products. Each of these things works together, so make sure you have the right people and processes in place to reap the benefits of your new marketing efforts and you will be sure to sell a lot more of your products.

To illustrate this point, let's move on to discuss the lifetime value of a customer...

The lifetime value of a customer

When I am consulting with business owners, one of the most important topics we can discuss is the lifetime value of a customer. This is absolutely one of the most critical keys to managing and growing a business. Yet as important as it is, it is rare that a local business owner can ever give me a number, and most have never even given serious thought to the concept.

If you do not know how much a customer is worth to your business, how can you know how much you should be willing to spend on your marketing efforts or whether your marketing is giving you a positive return on your investment? You can't. You cannot with any good-faith basis make a sound decision on how much to spend on your marketing campaign, and you cannot calculate the profitability of your campaign investment once it is finished.

This is unacceptable to business owners who want to maximize their success. I can completely understand that people become plumbers, hair stylists, massage therapists, doctors, attorneys, etc. because they enjoy working in those fields. And while these people may be the very best at what they do, the fact is most never give serious thought to an in-depth study of the marketing side of business. But it has to be done if you want your business to be as successful as it possibly can.

While this lack of experience in implementing and analyzing local marketing may be understandable, one cannot escape the fact that businesses that are able to understand and measure the lifetime value of their customers will have a significant advantage over businesses that ignore this crucial business metric. So, let's take a look at an example so that you can get started with examining the lifetime value of your customers.

For this example, I will use a massage therapist I recently helped in a nearby city. During our discussions, she said that she had an ad in the phone book that cost her thousands of dollars a year and she only received about 4 customers a year. Part of me thinks that she didn't really track where her customers came from but, on the other hand, phone book ads are dying and I have never spoken to a business owner that felt they received good value from phone book ads.

Due to her previous failed attempt at "marketing" she didn't believe that I could help her. Her logic was that if the phone book couldn't product results, why would the internet be any different? She was also worried that after a small upfront development charge, her ongoing marketing spend was going to be about $25 a month. Talk about having little faith!

So, this is where we discuss the true value of a customer. I explain that if she does only get 4 customers a year (using her numbers, the Google AdWords tool indicated that she would be getting more than that every month and now she is!), and she does a great job at a fair price, and just 1 of those 4 becomes a regular customer, she could make at least $1400 from that customer.

How did I arrive at that number? The therapist said that a regular customer will visit on average at least once every 3 months, quite often they will visit more but we need to be conservative. She also said that her tip was between $10 and $20 from good customers. So if she charges $60 an hour and gets just a $10 tip, that is $70 a visit.

Now that we have the revenue per visit, and the frequency of visits, it is easy to calculate minimal revenues of $280 a year. If the customer is receiving great service at a fair price they will keep coming back year after year. So over the course of 5 years, the customer is worth $1400 in revenues. If she makes all 4 new customers regular customers, then the numbers grow much higher. But the point is just *one customer a year* offers her a positive return on her investment.

When you are able to assign a value to a customer, suddenly the $25 a month spend as well as the initial investment in her new website and local listings (YouTube, Google, Bing, and Yahoo), looks cheap. Keep in mind that every city and every business type will have different projected numbers of customers and different costs of effectively marketing to that customer base. But the formula is always the same - projected revenue x the number of service opportunities x the length of customer retention.

It is only after you take the time to calculate the true value of your customers that you can devise a cost-effective marketing plan to reach those customers!

Now that you understand just how important a single customer can be, let's dive into how you can get your share of them...

Where are potential customers looking for local businesses?

If you want to get your share of new customers, you have to market where your customers are looking for your products and services. Before the advent of the internet, marketing options for local businesses were pretty straightforward. If they could afford an ad in the phone book, that was the first option. Some also used newspaper ads and radio. There were also billboards and magazines, but that was about it and those were not cheap.

Today, thankfully, business owners have many tools at their disposal and most are free or very affordable. All business owners have to do is understand what they are and how to use them strategically to grow their businesses.

So, where are potential customers looking for local businesses? Not the phone books! Phone book ads don't work as well as they used to, ask 20 businesses if they feel their phone book ads are cost effective and at least 19 (if not all 20) will give you a resounding "NO." Why is this? Well, the answer to that question is easy... people just don't use them like the used to in the past.

Phone books are going the way of VHS tapes and pagers. In fact, according to a 2011 statistic from Harris Interactive, approximately 70% of U.S. adults will "rarely or never" use phone books. Today they are choosing to use the internet as their primary tool to find contact information for local businesses. Keep in mind that this is an old statistic and today the decline is certainly to be even greater given the shift towards the internet and the rise in tablet and smart phone adoption.

Even Yellow Pages themselves are preparing for the downfall of the old fashioned phone book. They have publicly stated that they will derive 53% of their revenue from digital ad sales. One has no choice but to face the fact that digital advertising is the future. So, if you are going to be online, and you had better be if you want to survive in the marketplace, why not get the biggest bang for your buck rather than give it to Yellow Pages and the like?

Today, consumers are searching online for local stores and products. If you want to reach them, you need to establish a presence and provide relevant information. According to the Kelsey Group, 74% of internet users perform local searches. And ComScore research indicates that a staggering 90% of online commercial searches result in offline bricks and mortar purchases.

Similarly, Microsoft has offered up statistics that show 53 percent of all mobile searches on their search engine, Bing, are for local goods and services.

The takeaway to all of these numbers is that consumers are searching for local products and services online. If you want to reach these potential customers, you need to go where your customers are looking... you need to be online with a professional presence and giving your potential customers the information that they need to make a decision - the decision to choose your business!

Unfortunately, most local business owner just don't "get" the internet as a marketing tool...

Most local business owners just don't "get" the internet as a marketing tool

It's important to understand that marketing online isn't an option these days, it's a requirement for businesses that want to compete in the marketplace. As was discussed in the last chapter, customers are looking for local businesses ONLINE!

As important as it is to understand this, not every business is taking advantage of what amounts to the cheapest form of advertisement available. I have spoken to many business owners about why they don't have a website and their reasons are varied.

- Some just don't understand the internet.
- Some are skeptical because they get bombarded by sleazy companies calling them every other day trying to sell them some ridiculously expensive "package."
- Some do not believe that there is enough business in their niche to justify the costs.
- "I'm going to do it some day."
- Etc.

If this sounds like you, then you are reading the perfect book. By the end of this book, you will "get it" and you will be ready to get started. The reasons above are not valid justifications to miss out on all of the benefits available to you by using online marketing in a strategic and cost-effective way.

Incredibly, over half of all small businesses do not have a website. When I speak to business owners, the number one issue is the cost. Not surprisingly, these same business owners cannot tell me how much a website costs. Likewise, they cannot tell me the lifetime value of a customer. Most of them have preconceived notions and, honestly, do not want to be bothered with trying to understand. Fortunately, since you are reading this book, you are not one of them! At least you are open to new ideas and I applaud you for that.

While a website is not the total of your online marketing strategy, it is usually the first tactic that a local business owner should implement. Only 44% of local businesses have a website - good or bad. If you are one of the 44%, make sure that your website is current, provides useful information, and reflects well on your business. If you are in the 56% of local businesses that do not have a website, what are you waiting for? You are literally ignoring the 70% of people that will "rarely or never" use a phone book and instead will be looking online for your product or service. With so few local businesses actively engaged in online marketing of their business, you can not only compete, but chances are you can dominate your local market.

Do you need another reason to get your business online? Well how about the fact that 79% of Google searchers claim that they ignore paid advertising and only click on organic search results? In other words, good local SEO reaches more customers than paid online advertising.

How do you take advantage of this information?

> ➢ Make sure you have a professionally built website.
> ➢ Optimize your website for search.
> ➢ List your business and website in local online directories.
> ➢ Optimize your site for mobile devices.

> ➢ Create valuable content about your products and services, include reviews, and make sure it's easy for potential shoppers to locate your store or get information.

So, if almost all of your potential customers are looking online to find you, and your business...

> ➢ Is not there because you have no website;

> ➢ Not found due to a lack of search engine optimization;

> ➢ Or doesn't reflect well on your business.

Then you are 100% guaranteed that all of your potential customers that use the internet searching for local goods and services will be buying from your competitors instead of you.

Don't ignore your online marketing! With all of the tools available to you to help you grow your business, it is truly the biggest mistake that a local business can make...

The biggest mistake that a local business can make!

The biggest mistake that a local business can make, in my opinion, is ignoring their online marketing efforts. Many local business owners will tell me that they don't understand it or that they don't have time for it. Is it any wonder that, according to Bloomberg, 8 out of 10 entrepreneurs who start a business fails within the first 18 months? If you don't understand online marketing, find someone you trust and let them do it for you.

The two biggest excuses that local business owners will give for ignoring their online marketing are (1) cost and (2) lack of time.

Business owners will cite cost as an issue when they do not even know how much a website and related marketing services cost and with no idea as to the lifetime value of a customer. It is a "knee jerk" reaction to avoid confronting an issue that simply confuses them.

And when business owners say they don't have time, they are saying they don't have the time to make sure their business is a success instead of a failure. So, again, find someone you trust and let them help you.

Google, Yahoo, and Bing all give you free listings. YouTube allows you to post videos for free. Twitter accounts are free. Facebook accounts are free. Websites are very affordable - at least mine are. There are countless directories that give free listings... you just have to put up with the sales calls that come with the listings. But they are all FREE!

Business owners have never in history had access to such a multitude of opportunities and tools to help them build their brand and grow their business. It just takes time and training.

For local businesses, online marketing presents an unbeatable and extremely cost-effective opportunity to get more leads which will result in more customers. If you don't understand it, Google is your friend. Everything you need to know is available online for free. If you don't want to invest months into learning, or just prefer to focus on your core business (a very wise option), develop a relationship with a professional you can trust and start growing your business today!

By the end of this book, we will have discussed the most common tools available to you as a local business owner. Amazingly, if you could do the work yourself, they are almost all free or very inexpensive, yet business owners ignore the potential because it is confusing or time consuming, or both.

Take the time to understand the principles in this book and implement them or simply use them to evaluate any proposal you may receive and make a good financial decision as to whether or not certain marketing approaches will give you a positive return on your investment. But by all means, do not do what many local business owners do.

Do not simply ignore opportunities to grow your business...

Ignoring opportunities to grow your business

If you ignore opportunities to grow your business and your competition doesn't, you WILL be losing customers!

If you are like me, you probably get more sales calls in a day than you would like. My immediate reaction is to say, "I'm not interested, thanks" and then immediately hang up the phone. That's why I never use cold calling to try to grow my business. Business owners, like myself, have grown numb to sales calls. And, to be frank, in my opinion 99% of all the sales calls you get ARE A SCAM!

Let's face it, there are many companies out there that "scrape" phone numbers off the internet and use robo-calling to try and reach business owners in order to try to sell them some form of marketing - websites, SEO, etc. These companies have not done one bit of research on how they can help your business, but they are sure that you need their over-priced services.

As a side note, that is why I use highly targeted letters to generate more business. I take the time to research businesses for which I know for certain that I can add value. Often I will even capture the screen and highlight the problem, and offer to help with a very attractive offer.

With all of the shenanigans in this industry, the spammy phone calls, the false promises and the like, it is no wonder that the first inclination of business owners is to dismiss all offers for help with their marketing. It has become a conditioned response, and with very good reason. Business owners have become immune to the tactics of these dubious companies.

It is not that businesses do not care that they are at a competitive disadvantage. Likewise, it is not because they all have as much business as they can handle and don't want any more. Business owners ignore opportunities to grow their business simply due to the fact that they have become so inundated with people trying to sell them something. Business owners don't know these people, and justifiably, they just say "No" to everyone without thinking about the offer.

Here is the take away point - become informed, by all means be cautious, but be receptive to new ideas. Using the value of a customer, examine the offers being pitched to you and logically determine if there is any way your business could benefit from what you are being offered. Then take your time and do your own research. Call around and get some quotes from a local vendor you can build a relationship with. This way you can do a cost to benefit analysis and see if your investment in that area would be wise. You don't have to make a hasty decision from some random guy on the phone, but rather make a sound business decision based on solid data. Keep in mind that the vendor doesn't have to be local to you to deliver quality solutions, they just need to be reputable and deliver value.

As an example, since this is one of the fulfillment services that I sometimes offer, I am sure that you receive many calls from random "phone guys" wanting to sell you a website, or a website redesign, or internet marketing. Buying from these calls would likely be a very costly mistake. But that doesn't mean that a business couldn't do some research on the benefits of a website if you don't have one. Or a redesign if your site is old and looks "dated" or maybe a redesign if your current site isn't mobile compatible. Then take a few minutes to call a few companies that do web design, compare their prices for web design and hosting plus maintenance, and get your business online at a fair price.

Knowing what I know, it is staggering to me that any business wouldn't have a website. Which is why I try to educate customers and let them decide if an investment in their business is justified. I don't try to sell. I have found that if I educate business owners, local marketing sells itself. But if you are a business owner that is never receptive to new ideas and trying new things, you are selling your business short.

To wrap things up, don't let yourself get turned off to new things that can help to grow your business. Instead take the ideas and do your due diligence and see if the investment makes good financial sense for your business. Not to be redundant, but it needs to be said again and again, if you ignore opportunities to grow your business and your competition doesn't, you WILL be losing customers!

The basic online marketing plan for a local business

By now a rather compelling case has been presented for online marketing as a tool for growing your business. Without getting ahead of ourselves, let's have a look at what a simple marketing plan may look like. Every business and every market is unique. There is no "one plan fits all" when it comes to local marketing. A plan for a plumber in Miami Florida will be different from a plumber in Bartow Florida due to the amount of competition. As a rule, the larger the city, the tougher the competition and the more difficult it will be to rank high in the search engines.

However, regardless of the market, most online marketing campaigns will have most of the following:

- ➢ A professionally built website that is responsive to mobile devices.
- ➢ The major local listings (Google, Yahoo, and Bing).
- ➢ A YouTube account with videos targeting your type of business. These videos will also be linked to your local listings and will be pointing to your website.
- ➢ Listings in local directories such as Yelp, Merchant Circle, Angie's List, etc.
- ➢ A facebook local business page.

There is a lot of work that goes into these items, but these are the foundation for your online marketing initiative.

Later a business might start using Twitter, paid ads, email marketing, and other tactical items in order to improve organic search engine rankings, customer engagement, and to get more customers!

Now it is time for us to dive into the details and begin understanding what should go into the building of each of these items and why. There is a big difference between telling a business owner that they need a "professionally built website that is responsive to mobile devices" and explaining what makes for a great website and why it is crucial that it is responsive to mobile devices.

So, let's start with understanding the impact of your website presentation...

Ugly websites hurt your business

Your website is the foundation of your local marketing efforts, so getting this part right is crucial to your marketing success - the ability to drive sales. In order to help you get it right, we will be looking at several requirements for your website. The first being its visual appeal.

Whether it is an existing website or you will be creating a new one, make sure that it looks clean and professionally built. Your business will be judged by it!

This is one area where business owners really hurt themselves. They either have an old out-dated website that looks bad or a new one that wasn't professionally built with the customer in mind and looks bad. In fact, a study was conducted by BrightLocal which showed that 75 percent of consumers will base their opinion of a local business on its website.

> ➢ 66% feel that a nice clean professional website gives a local business more credibility.

> ➢ 9% of those surveyed would refuse to do business with a business that had a bad or ugly website.

Most business owners I talk to do not realize how powerful an impression visitors can have of a company based on their website. They think that if they display their address, phone number, hours, etc. that people will call. But as seen by the BrightLocal study, that isn't always the case.

That's when I explain what is known in psychology as "The Halo Effect." This is a psychological term which essentially means that people actually do judge a book by its cover. This phenomenon has been well documented in all areas of life - politics, judicial proceedings, classroom studies, advertising and many more.

It is a well documented fact that attractive people, for example, get convicted less frequently and receive lighter sentences than those deemed to be less attractive. Likewise, more attractive politicians usually win elections. The analysis of this area of human behavior is quite interesting and can be quite beneficial to a business owner and I would encourage you to do some further reading on it.

At this point you are probably wondering what this has to do with your website. Well, the same principle holds true for your website. You are being judged by it and very often customers are deciding between your business and your competition based on it. Don't take this to mean that you need a "Disney-esque" website to create a positive first impression. But you do need a clean layout that looks professional with content that is well written.

So, if you are one of the many local businesses that haven't touched their websites in years, you had better take a look at it and decide if it gives the impression you want consumers to have of your business. Likewise, if you saw one of those commercials from companies like 1&1, Intuit, or Vistaprint and decided that was the way to go, you need to take a long hard look at the website to see what impression it will make.

The sad thing is that business owners fall victim to these types of companies due to unscrupulous affiliate marketers. If you search Google for, say, 1&1 you will get tons of rave reviews because affiliate marketers will get a commission for everyone that clicks the links from their spammy sites to sign up at these DIY site builders.

Business owners more often than not find out, often surprisingly to them, that their quick and easy website really isn't all that quick and easy and it doesn't really help their business. I find that I often have to take time to educate business owners about the difference between having a website and having a high quality site that ranks high in the search engines for the market in which they are attempting to compete.

(As a side note, trying to do proper on-page SEO on sites built with some of these tools is next to impossible!)

I'm not saying that a person can't build a nice professional site with these tools. But I am saying that it is very few people that actually have the time and know-how to get their content written for maximum search engine love while conveying a positive impression to potential customers. Also, most do not know how to size and crop their images for site performance as well as looking great. Have you ever been to a site that has several pictures and loads very slowly? Chances are the images are just too large. A site that is too slow will make customers leave in a hurry!

So, take an honest look at your website. Is it appealing? Does it give customers a favorable impression of your company? Does it present your products and services in a clear and convincing manner? Does it automatically resize to all screen sizes and look great on tablets and other mobile devices?

If you cannot answer a resounding "yes" to every question, maybe it is time for a facelift.

Here is a tip, ask local web design companies for an assessment. Most will do it for free in order to potentially get your business if a redesign is in order. Compare the findings from a couple of companies and see if they are saying the same things. Compare the detail of the proposals.

Also, have friends and family members tell you what they think of your website. With a small investment in time, you can come to a good fact-based decision on the appeal of your website and determine if an update is in order.

Your website is a 24 hour a day salesman

Your website is a salesman on steroids. This is a very good thing because it will work hard for you for pennies a day. But, like having a poor salesman, it can also hurt your business. The difference is that unlike an individual, the effects can be magnified because your website has a much greater reach than a single individual. This is why getting your website done correctly is vital to your marketing success.

Like a salesman, your website is there to produce results. When companies are attempting to sell you a website or other marketing services, they will give you many reasons to have a website or online marketing plan. Branding, disseminating information, etc., these are not practical reasons for having a website. They can lead up to the reason, but they are not THE reason.

Let's be very clear... the only reason for a business to have a website is to, ultimately, drive sales. There are many ways that this end result can be accomplished - better visibility, great content that makes customers want to call or visit your business, or just having the basic information that someone is looking for at the time that they are looking.

Regardless of how we get there, the end result is that your website, like any form of advertisement exists to make sales. Without accomplishing its job, your website doesn't justify its investment. Your website isn't something that is there to keep your name out there in the ubiquitous world wide web. It's not something you invest in because everyone else is doing it. No, you make the investment because you expect a positive return on your investment.

Given your website's potential reach, every website should be viewed as a "super" salesman. Unlike a single salesperson, your website is there 24 hours a day, 7 days a week. The biggest difference between it and a person is that your website is ALWAYS there, working for pennies a day, and it can literally market to thousands of people.

As we know with super heroes, with great power comes great responsibility, right? If you hired a salesperson and that individual made a poor impression on a customer, it would cost your business a little bit but it would hardly, in most cases, be devastating. However, make a mistake on your website and the effects are multiplied. It could significantly impact your bottom line. That is why it is so important to hire a professional to design your website and to help you get it ranked in the search engines.

Where do businesses go wrong? Often it is in not designing your website with your target customer in mind. Some business owners want to be cute and gimmicky with their website. They want dancing bears and music that blares when visitors land on the home page. While there are situations where that may be the exact design that is called for, would that really be the case for a professional insurance company? No! Likewise there are a number of businesses that will build their own sites with no training and end up with a site that looks like a junior high computer science project. Is that the image that any professional company would like to project? Again, the answer is a resounding No!

This is why a company that does bounce house rentals will get a five page website for a lot less than a professional accounting or law firm. A company has to invest in their "super salesman" and dress him/her in a way that will make the right impression on their target audience. Some business needs will call for unusual and distinctive designs while others will call for a more elegant look and feel. Build your site to be a vehicle to drive sales, not to be amusing. Your site should be an extension of sales, not a form of entertainment. This is another potentially huge mistake that a business will make. Whether they "under dress" their electronic salesperson or "over dress" it, they are missing the target.

This is where a good web design firm will help considerably. Helping you when you plan your site and keeping your typical customer in mind. Often business owners think of people as some generic group. They want to appeal to the city of whatever. But you have to focus on the customer that is likely to use your products or services and design with them in mind.

And in a world that is rapidly going mobile via iPads, other tablets, and smart phones, your super salesman has to be responsive to the needs of everyone...

Why having a mobile ready website is important

Just about everyone that has a phone number listed anywhere online gets sales calls just about every day from someone wanting to sell mobile websites. When you look at statistics, the case appears to be compelling - and it certainly is as we will see below, but separate mobile sites are a dying breed.

In 2013, the amount of time that people using mobile devices (smart phones and tablets) spent interacting with retail websites exceeded the amount of time spent by consumers using desktops and laptops - 55% to 45%. Looking at the mobile stat in a little more detail, smart phone users comprised 44% of retail internet time, and tablets came in second with an 11% share.

ComScore also reports that mobile users, while shopping, took a picture of a product (23%), sent a text or called family or friends about a product (17%), or sent a picture of a product to family and friends (17%).

ComScore research also shows that 64% of smart phone owners in Q2 2013 used a mobile web browser to research product features, and 59% used a mobile web browser to find a store location.

By now some of you are thinking, "but I'm not a retailer." Well, local searches in general, using mobile devices, is projected to exceed desktop searches by 2015 (eMarketer). And, when mobile users search for local information, 70 percent connect with the business (Televox).

Likewise, websites that are not optimized for mobile devices have a 24% higher "bounce" rate from mobile visitors (Televox).

By now it should be clear that mobile access to your website cannot be ignored. If your site isn't mobile ready your customers will have a negative experience and you will be losing customers as well as money.

But unless you have very unique requirements, don't fall for the separate mobile website scam. Separate sites were fine in the "good old days" but in the past few years the trend has been to build sites with responsive frameworks. One site that does it all. One development charge, and one hosting and maintenance charge. You have one site to maintain and it renders well on all devices. While occasionally there may be some things that don't render well, that is coded around. By choosing to build your website using responsive technologies, you will be tapping into a rapidly growing market segment at virtually no extra cost for development!

Choosing a marketing consultant

By now you have seen the value of local marketing and you should be convinced that the foundation of your local marketing is a great mobile responsive website. Getting this cornerstone of your marketing plan in place, and getting it done right is crucial to your local marketing success.

I debated whether this chapter should come here or at the end of the book. I decided it should come here because we have spent a lot of time discussing the importance of your website and getting help with building it is probably running through your head right now. So it is essential for me to make a very significant point right now.

If you need help with your local marketing, don't just hire a "web guy" make sure that your consultant is really a local marketing expert! Your local marketing plan, as you will see in the rest of this book, is much more than just a website. It is about using your website along with YouTube, local business listings, facebook, etc. where it makes sense and will add value to your business.

I have had business owners tell me that their nephew or some friend from their church, or whatever can build them a website and they don't need any help from my company. That is because they don't see the big picture.

There is a reason that big corporations spend millions of dollars every year on advertising, and there is a reason that they hire professionals and not kids in the neighborhood. They know that marketing is complex and requires a professional skill set just like any other profession.

Local marketing is the same, just on a much smaller scale. But just because the scope is smaller, doesn't mean that you don't need some guidance. Fortunately, you purchased this book and are on your way to seeing the big picture and you will be able to effectively implement a successful local marketing plan.

You will be able to implement this plan yourself if you have the time, but if you don't, you have in your hands everything you will need to know when a consultant is being honest and when he is hyping something just to sell you more services.

Bottom line, if you choose to get help with your local marketing, choose a professional! Ask for proof of their work. Ask for websites they have done, look at the rankings for these sites and their associated keywords, look at videos they have delivered for other clients, and look at the facebook page. After you have seen these and are satisfied with the quality, check a couple of references.

I suggest that you put more weight of your evaluation into the quality of the samples you are shown rather than the references. No one is going to give you a reference that will say bad things.

How to compare website design offers

The value in having a website for your business has been made pretty obvious by now. If not, go back to the beginning and start reading again. Your website is the cornerstone of your local business marketing efforts and one of the most important investment decisions you can make.

So you contact a couple of web design firms and get proposals. How do you compare the offers to get the best value for your money? The tendency among business owners is to compare based on price, but that isn't the best way.

Not all proposals are created equal. You have to take the time to understand what is included and choose the proposal that is going to deliver a great website that meets your specific business requirements while showing you the positive return and value you will derive from your investment. **Plus you need to ensure great support after the site is delivered.**

Cost is not as important as getting a solution that meets your business objectives and delivers a positive return on your investment. What good is a cheap website if it doesn't drive sales and business growth?

Unfortunately, most business owners want to know how much a website costs before the design company even has a chance to understand requirements. I once had a business call and ask me to come talk about a new website for their business. As soon as I got there, they wanted me to do a full presentation and give them a cost. That's like asking an architect to give you a house design without discussing your needs first. It was a complete waste of their time and a complete waste of my time. Don't be one of these business owners. You have to take the time to explain your goals, the results you expect, and the features you want (among other things) before your design company can offer a solution. And it is the solution that will ultimately determine cost.

When I go on an initial client meeting, I don't bring a stack of generic literature with rate sheets so that I can "close" a business deal. I go with a notepad and a pen. I want to understand the customer's requirements so that I can offer a solution that will match 100% with the client's goals.

Cost is important, nobody wants to spend more money than they need to - but getting the right solution that will deliver a positive return on your investment is even more important. To get the right solution, you need to spend time on the goals and objectives of your website.

1. Make sure your requirements are met in the proposal in an affordable way

The first step in evaluating website proposals is to make sure that the company you choose has understood your requirements and will deliver them with your finished product. A good dialogue is the key to gathering your requirements and ensuring you are getting the right solution offered for your needs. If you just need to display a few pages of information about your products or services, you don't need a $20,000 fully flash driven "Disney" styled website.

If you have the money and you want a lavish site for branding reasons or just because you can, great. But your website needs to be built around your business needs. In most cases, there is no need for the "Mona Lisa" of designs, just a professional site with a pleasing visual layout that will give your customers the information they need to choose your business. This decision is up to you. Your design company should be asking you for your expectations so that those expectations can be met.

2. Are they going to help you make good decisions on your online marketing based on years of experience in the business?

This goes hand-in-hand with the first point. Not only should you get your requirements met, but your web design firm needs to have enough experience in business to help you make good decisions as to what those requirements should be. With some firms, if the customer says that they need dancing bears on the home page with music that automatically plays when a person comes to the site, they will say, "OK" and gladly charge you for it. But what your web design firm should do is ask why you feel that dancing bears is needed and ascertain if the added value will justify the added costs. Likewise they should have enough experience to point out that a very significant number of people will immediately navigate away from a page that starts blaring music at them.

You, as the customer and business owner, of course, have the final say. But it is important that your firm has experience and can offer up more cost effective solutions when it is appropriate. As a business owner, I always love to make more money. But I can't in good conscience sell a customer something that I don't believe in without giving the customer alternatives based on my years of experience. If you never get any alternatives proposed, you are probably not getting the best value for your money.

3. Who will be doing the actual work and will they be there to support you?

There are many companies that offer low rates and outsource the project and you never hear from them again or when they do, they have to charge high rates because of their outsourcing arrangement. Make sure that the firm building your site is building the site in-house and will be there to support you after your site goes live.

4. Are they going to do free small updates for specials for Valentine's Day, Mother's Day, Christmas, etc?

This assumes that you have a reasonable hosting and maintenance agreement. If you choose to "pay as you go" you cannot expect free updates. But your website development company should offer this service as part of their maintenance and support options. This does not mean a complete re-design! But you should be able to highlight special offers about 4 times a year for free. Every business should be doing this to entice customers to come back. Your website is never finished - you should be updating it regularly. If not, you might be charged up to $200 an hour... yes, some companies charge this and some charge even more.

Ask about rates for website changes before you let someone build your website. I have seen cases where it was actually cheaper to start over from scratch and rebuild a website than it was to continue to pay some of the ridiculous hosting and maintenance fees that some companies try to charge. As a business owner, you have to respect the fact that your web design company has a family to feed, just like you do. But I have seen too many cases where businesses were being charged $200 -

$400 a month for essentially nothing. The business owners didn't know any better and they were taken advantage of by unscrupulous vendors. But you are armed with the information in this book and this will not be you!

5. Is your new website going to be mobile compatible?

These days the need for mobile compatible websites is beyond debate and the days of having separate sites for mobile devices has gone the way of the dinosaur. Do not invest in a website that is not responsive to mobile devices. No exceptions.

6. Will they optimize your site for search engines or is it an extra cost?

Having a website that isn't optimized for search engines is not a wise investment in your business. This doesn't mean that your site will automatically be #1 on Google, but the foundation for SEO is proper on-site optimization and it should be included with your site at no extra cost. But some firms just want to "hit and run" and will ignore this very important step. You ask for a website so they give you one. They don't care if it ranks well or has proper SEO built into it from the beginning. They have your check and they are gone.

While the search engines are beginning to devalue some of the importance of on-page SEO, it is still an important area of website design. The content has to be written correctly, the META data has to be there, and images have to be named correctly and given good titles. Skip this step in the beginning and you will be paying again later for something that should have been included from the start. Not to mention that you lose the chance to get better search engine rankings faster.

Get these six things right and you will be in fine shape

There are many smaller issues to consider, but if you make sure that your vendor is doing these six things mentioned above, you will be way ahead of most local business owners looking to have a website built. When you understand and apply these criteria along with price estimates in a true "apples to apples" comparison, you will end up with a great website that will deliver value for your investment dollars.

How much should a website cost?

That is an almost impossible question to ask without knowing the number of pages and the complexity of each page. The cost will vary based on the "bells and whistles" you ask for. If you have done a good analysis of your proposals based on the criteria I have outlined above, you will know if they are fair. If you only get two proposals and they are far apart, get a third proposal or pay to get an unbiased second opinion from a marketing consultant you can trust. Shameless plug, I will evaluate your proposals for a very reasonable fee!

Should I just let a national company handle all of this for me?

The short answer is "NO!" But you probably want more of an explanation. This chapter is in here as a service to prevent business owners from making the mistake of using one of these national companies. It also serves as a "breakaway" strategy for those unfortunate enough to have already entered into a contract with these companies.

The problem with using a national company for your website and online marketing is that THEY own your website content and you are stuck with them at an unacceptable price point.

There are several major national companies that offer websites and online marketing to businesses and they all, without exception, charge way too much for what you are getting. SuperMedia, Intuit (now Homestead), Yellowbook (now Hibu), etc. all offer variations on this service. So let's just look at one, Supermedia (which in my opinion isn't as bad as Hibu), and see what kind of experience a business owner is likely to receive.

If you are a business owner that has a website built by SuperMedia, you understand the need for online marketing for your business. That is a good thing and you should feel proud of yourself as you are well ahead of many of your competitors. But if you are currently a SuperMedia customer, chances are you are not happy with your experience. In fact surveys show that over 80% of their current customers:

1. Feel that they are paying too much.

2. Think they are not getting the level of service their business deserves.

3. And/or would cancel their contracts immediately if they were allowed.

Why is this? Well, here is what you get with SuperMedia:

➢ Websites start at $59.50 per month but many businesses pay more.

➢ You are locked into a contract!

➢ The websites are all built with templates which makes many of them look alike. So much for a unique brand!

➢ You are buying from a salesperson that is getting a fat commission from the sale regardless of your success. After that you are dealing with a huge corporation. Nobody is invested in your success!

➢ Go to complaintsboard.com and read the complaints.

➢ Go to ripoffreport.com and read the complaints.

➢ Go to http://mythreecents.com/reviews/supermedia and read the complaints.

➢ Go to http://www.scambook.com/company/view/117576/Supermedia and read the complaints.

The bottom line is that I have never met a person who said they felt they have received good value for their money by using these website services! I'm sure that there are some, but they are, by far, the minority of their customer base.

You can have any reputable web company create a new site for less and get better service and better value. Again, there are good local web design companies out there and there are some bad ones. Take the time to make sure you are getting a good one! Don't just trade one problem for another.

Here is what you would need to have performed to do a SuperMedia (or any of these national companies) replacement:

➢ Create a new website with the same number of pages and rewrite the content since SuperMedia owns your website content

➢ Purchase replacement photos where Super Media owns them.

➢ Purchase a domain name if you decide not to pay the Super Media "domain release" charge or help you transfer your domain name should you want to pay the Super Media "domain release" charge. If you are not at the end of your contract, a new domain is the way to go. This allows you to get everything up and running with no interruption to your web presence. Then just do a forward of your old domain name to your new one after your contract is finished.

Make sure that you choose a company that will do it with NO LONG-TERM CONTRACTS! You should be free to cancel at any time. You want a company that knows you are staying with them because you are delighted with their service, not because you got stuck with a contract. Plus, you will be dealing with someone local that has a vested interest in seeing you succeed.

But don't delay, now is the time to get your replacement plan started. You don't want to have a gap in your advertising between canceling your contract and getting your replacement site built and ranked.

Youtube

YouTube is a tool that every business, local or not, should be taking advantage of for their marketing efforts. But unless you have a cat that can rock out on a piano, you need to have your expectations set correctly.

While you probably won't have your videos go viral, people will view your videos. No matter the size of the city or the type of business, I have never had a video with no views. In some smaller markets the view count can be low, but even if 10 people are looking for your type of business in your city, you certainly want them to find YOUR business. YouTube is the second largest search engine in the world, your business should take advantage of that and have a YouTube channel.

Another compelling reason for investing in your YouTube channel is that the videos can be good citations (mentions of your business) that can help improve the rankings of your website, Google+, and Bing listings. Google+ as well as Bing allow you to link to your videos. Use this to your advantage! And if you put some work into it, your videos can even rank for your search terms. That is a double win for you and your business.

The icing on the cake? According to a survey by Yodle, only about 10% of small businesses use ANY form of social media marketing or online advertising. You want to be there because there is a very good chance that your competition is not.

Now that you are thoroughly convinced that you want to be a leader in your market and get your fair share of the YouTube traffic for your city and type of business, let's look at what you need to do to be successful.

First, get started! Remember that you are ahead of your competition and you do not need a video that would make George Lucas proud. Your goal isn't an academy award, it is a simple professional video that represents your business and your products and/or services well.

Create interesting videos

Again, you aren't trying to be cute and have a viral video viewed by millions, you are creating something that will be interesting enough that potential customers will watch it and then call your company.

A "viral" video would be almost worthless for a local business anyway. Sure you might get a little local buzz from it, but the chances of a high school kid in Beijing needing a plumber in Lakeland Florida is pretty small.

Think about who your target customer is and the information that they would need to decide that your company is the one they should be using. Then create videos that deliver that information to your potential customers.

Optimize your videos for search

If your videos cannot be found, they are not much use to you and your business. Make sure that YouTube and the search engines know what your video is about. This is done by "optimizing" your videos for search.

The first item in your optimization efforts is to use your keywords in your YouTube video title. If your company is a hair salon in Atlanta, use a title similar to "Atlanta hair salon for perfect cuts" so that it is obvious what your video is about. Don't just use your company name. People searching for a hair salon in Atlanta probably don't know your company name so you don't want to optimize around that. You may have one video optimized for your company name, but use your videos as tools to get search traffic.

The second item is the YouTube video description. Always link to your website as the first entry of the description. Then write a nice 200 word description with your keywords mentioned a couple of times. You don't want to mention it too many times, the search engines are smarter than you are and they will ignore your videos. But a couple of times is fine and needs to be done to help the search engines know what your video is about. The last thing you should do is put your company name, address, and phone number at the end of the description to get the full value of the citation and help your website rank better in the search engines.

Third, YouTube lets you add keywords so use them liberally. The more the better up to a point. Up to 10 keywords is plenty.

Lastly, under the "advanced" settings, be sure to enter your address.

These few items are by no means the only variables in used to rank videos. However, they are the basics that everyone should do. And if your competition isn't doing them or isn't even on YouTube, these will put you well ahead of others in your city and niche.

What types of videos can you put on YouTube?

You can create videos that describe your products and services, videos that demonstrate your products, helpful videos that educate consumers and build your credibility, and you can have customers give reviews of your business. The only limit is your imagination.

One tip that I see very few business owners doing is creating videos that they can also embed on their website's "about us" page that thank people for showing interest in your company.

Be sure to brand your channel

This is really just as simple as creating a custom background with a nice image that represents your business. Make sure it is clean, professional, and makes use of your company colors. Using the default YouTube background does not give your business credibility.

The bottom line is that if you are a local business owner and you're not leveraging YouTube, you're missing out on a great FREE marketing platform.

Google, Bing, and Yahoo

These are the "big 3" in terms of local business listings. When you do a local search in Google for a local business type or service ("plumbers in Tampa" for example), you will get a listing of local businesses and a "maps" listing with seven businesses. Being in this "7 pack" or above it is the goal of every local business.

In this book, I will refer to Google since they dominate the search engine market. But do keep in mind that the information in the book applies to all three major search engines. The steps you use for ranking your business in Google will apply to Bing and Yahoo as well.

You should also know that Bing supplies the search results for Yahoo, so there are really only two search engines of any consequence to worry about - Google and Bing. That does not mean you shouldn't claim a Yahoo local business listing, it is still good to get.

NOTE: As this book was going to press, Google announced the launch of Google "My Business" which will replace Google+ local business listings. The concepts for ranking and optimizing your listing are the same it is just a change to the user interface. That is why this book focuses on the concepts and not a paint-by-numbers approach.

For businesses that already have a Google+ local listing, your account will be transitioned over soon. For new business listings, let's get started.

Again, due to the nature of the internet - rapid change - this book will not walk you through the steps with pictures because any images printed today could likely change, as Google just did. Plus, it really isn't very difficult.

Go to http://www.google.com/mybusiness and sign up for a Google account if you do not have one already. If this link ever changes, just go to Google and search for "adding a Google my business local business listing" and you will be sure to easily find the signup link.

One other note, in some cases, especially for established businesses, there will already be an unclaimed local business listing. In this case, you will not be creating a listing but rather claiming one. Either way, there are some general rules you will need to follow in order to make your listing stand above the rest.

Start by gathering your business information

Google, Bing, and Yahoo will all ask for most of this information:

- ✓ Legal business name

- ✓ Address

- ✓ Primary phone number

- ✓ Fax number (optional)

- ✓ Toll-free number (optional)

- ✓ Website

- ✓ Category (e.g. butcher, baker, candle stick maker)

- ✓ Email address

- ✓ Business descriptions – one brief and one detailed

- ✓ Operating Hours

- ✓ Payment types accepted

- ✓ Year founded (or years in business)

- ✓ Associations/ certifications

- ✓ Languages spoken

- ✓ Number of employees

- ✓ Social media links (facebook, twitter, Google+)

- ✓ Service area/distance you will cover

- ✓ Brands carried

- ✓ License number

- ✓ Insured/bonded status

- ✓ 5 YouTube video links

- ✓ 10 images

Your listing must be complete and accurate

Be sure that your business name, address, and phone number (NAP) are correct and be sure that you are consistent later when we get to doing citations (mentions elsewhere on the internet - this will be in an upcoming chapter) for your business. For example, if your address is 123 West Main Street, consistently use the exact spellings in EVERY citation. Do not abbreviate "West" as "W" or abbreviate "Street" to "St" **unless you do that EVERYWHERE**. However you decide, "123 W Main St" or 123 West Main Street," do it that way every time.

It is important to add the URL of your website in your listing to help Google know what your business is about and to help Google deliver the best possible search results. The goal isn't really to help Google, it is to help you, so do it!

Fill out every field as completely as possible. Where Google lets you upload images, upload about 10. Be sure to name these with keywords that describe your products or services. If you are a hair salon in Lakeland Florida, one picture should be titled "lakeland-hair-salon.jpg" (or whatever file extension you are using), one should be "lakeland-beauty-salon.jpg' etc. Do this for all your products and services as well as one with your business name.

For Bing, be sure to add your videos. For Google your YouTube channel will be linked when you access it from your Google profile.

All other information, operating hours, payment types accepted, etc. needs to be as complete as possible. Do not skimp on the details. Your Google listing is too important.

Select the most appropriate business category for your business

Again, there will be some differences between Google and Bing, as of this writing, Google only allows one category and Bing will allow up to five. Regardless, be sure to select the most appropriate one(s) for your business.

Verify your listing

Once you are done, you will have to verify your listing to prove that you are indeed the owner of the business. This is almost always done by postcard to prove that you really are at the location you say you are and to prevent fraudulent listings. If you get lucky and have a phone option, by all means do it, don't let yourself wait for 2 weeks on a postcard.

Yahoo, on the other hand, makes verification easy. You will have the opportunity to verify via phone and in some cases via text message.

The next steps

The next step is to create a strong presence across the web. Google is very good at aggregating information from all over the web and will use that information to rank your business. This means that information about your business on third-party sites should be consistent (exactly the same) as the information you used for these "big 3" listings. The good news is that since you just did these primary listings you should have all of this information on hand for building your third-party listings that will build out your web presence.

Citations

Citations are mentions of your business across the web. For a local business, citations are the single biggest factor in how well you rank. But you really only want to invest your time in building out your web presence on quality citation sources. You want to build as many as you can as long as they are reputable sources.

Since there are literally hundreds of places to add your business listing, set a goal to do a couple every day and you can do a hundred or so over a few months. Once you achieve the ranking you want, you can stop until you notice that your ranking is slipping. Then you can add a few more.

I suggest that, for a new website, you start out fairly slowly and build a few the first couple of weeks, say 10, then ramp up to as many as you want. With only about 200 reasonably good sources for your citations, you don't have to go crazy all at once.

Be warned however that building citations is very tedious work and takes time. You have to think of this time as an investment in your business. An investment that will pay off once your site moves up the rankings.

You can also hire someone to take care of this for you. Shameless plug, I have an offshore team that can do this for about $2 per citation depending upon how many you order at one time.

Start with the best sources

Using the same information you collected previously for your Google, Bing, and Yahoo listings, here are some of the better sources for your citations:

- Brownbook.net

- Citysearch.com

- Citysquares.com

- Foursquare.com

- Hotfrog.com

- Insiderpages.com

- Kudzu.com

- Local.com

- Manta.com

- Mapquest.com

- Merchantcircle.com

- Mojopages.com

- Superpages.com

- Whitepages.com

- Yellowbot.com

- Yellowpages.com

- Yellowbook.com

- Yelp.com

Never pay to be listed in a directory! Be careful, these change all the time. If you find that one is no longer free, just move on to the next one.

Ramping up the volume

When you have added your company listing to all of the major citation sources, you can find more by doing a search on Google with your competitions phone number. Take your top 2 or 3 competitors (based on search engine rankings, not who you think is your main competition) and put their phone number in the Google search box and you will get tons of listings for where you can add a citation for your business.

Many of these places you probably have never heard of before. But since you found them using Google, you know for a fact that Google knows about them!

facebook for local businesses

facebook can be a great marketing tool for any business of any size in any industry. Where some social media platforms, like Twitter, may be better suited for larger companies and for brand building, facebook may actually be better for local businesses than larger ones. How many times have you been on facebook to engage with Ford or Sears?

So, as a blanket statement since there is always the exception that proves the rule, if you have a local business, facebook should be a key component of your local marketing strategy.

The great thing about facebook, like most of the tools I have highlighted throughout this book, is it is FREE to use to grow your online presence. They do offer facebook ads which cost real out-of-pocket cash, and after you have done everything else in this book, I would encourage you to test them out. But for now, if it's free, it's for me (and you!).

"Free" doesn't mean that it isn't going to take some work. facebook marketing does require a small investment of your time in order to be successful. You cannot just try to sell, you have to use the platform to "engage" with your customers.

Create your local business page

This book won't walk you through the creation of a local business page. It is simple and facebook already has resources that will always be current whereas any attempt I could make may be rendered obsolete at any time that facebook wishes to make a change.

To get started, go to *https://www.facebook.com/pages/create* and choose "Local Business or Place" and fill in everything asked. This will be easy because you still have the list of information about your company from before, right?

Do make sure that you create a nice professional background image. Remember, people will judge your business by the smallest of items.

Engaging with your followers

Now that you have a business page set up, it's time to start interacting and growing your followers. First, share more than just your sales pitch. If you never share anything interesting, your followers will just ignore your posts and you won't add too many new followers.

1. Share interesting news about your business. If you sponsor a softball team, mention that and how they are doing. If you are attending a trade show, share some of the interesting things you see. You should have a passion for your business, share it. People need to see that you care about more than selling them something!

2. Share interesting news about your community. If you know that there is a fundraiser for a band trip, share it. Help get the word out for events in the community.

3. Use pictures. Whether for your products and services or for your informational posts, add pictures to make your posts more interesting and to help them stand out.

4. Share your specials. Now that you have been sharing other news and interesting items, you can start selling to your followers. If you want to be able to track the success of your facebook marketing, post a code word or phrase that people have to mention in order to get the special. Also, make your offer compelling enough to drive traffic to your business. Buy one get one free is going to get more response than 5% off!

5. Make it easy for people to contact you. When you do post your specials, consider including your phone number. I know it is easy for people to find it if they click to the page, but why make them have to click anything? Easier is better for your customer conversions.

Get your facebook URL out there

Don't just put your business address and phone number on your business cards and other marketing materials. Make sure that you put your facebook URL on everything as well.

A facebook page for every location

If you have multiple legitimate physical locations, create a page for each one. This is good for SEO and it's good for customer engagement. Different locations will likely have different local community news that you can use for customer engagement.

You may not have time for managing multiple facebook pages, so get help if you need to, but don't ignore a chance to connect at a local level.

Twitter

Twitter is the last of the "big four" social media tools available for owners of small businesses (YouTube, Google+, and facebook being the other three). Two others, Pinterest and Instagram, are also growing in popularity and should be on every business owner's radar.

However, this book will stop with Twitter, and it will be a rather brief stop at that. According to a BrightLocal study, out of twelve marketing channels, Twitter had the lowest return on investment. Please do not take that to mean that Twitter is not a useful tool. When used properly, Twitter is a great marketing tool! It is fantastic! But the first word in the title of this book is "Practical" for a reason.

If you have time after doing the other items mentioned, by all means get started with Twitter and grow your brand by establishing yourself as an expert in your field and engaging with your customers with another of the many free tools available to you. But first, be sure that you have done everything else right.

Why Twitter?

After facebook, Twitter is the next most popular social media platform. If you are not familiar with Twitter, it is known as a "micro-blogging" platform due to its limitation of 140 characters or less for your messages.

Twitter can be an effective marketing tool under the right scenarios. But in order to be effective, business owners need to be engaging and sharing useful information. Also, realize that while it may build your brand and your credibility, it might not provide the ROI you are hoping for compared to your investment in time.

When would I use Twitter?

Twitter is to be used after all of the other strategies outlined in this book have been implemented. Then it is up to you to decide if the effort required is worth it for you and your business. The only way to know is to give it an honest try and see what your return is and if you feel like it is worth it to you.

Good examples of when Twitter makes sense

Here are a few examples of the wise use of Twitter. Again, any business can benefit to some degree, but these are examples of where Twitter can really pay off for a business.

If I were a "small" hotel in NYC, Orlando, Los Angeles, etc., I would use Twitter. People are coming from all over the country and I would be able to engage with them and it could drive room reservations.

One example I recently read about was a trendy popular food truck in LA that changed locations frequently. They have a loyal following and they use Twitter to let their customers know where to find them. This is a great example of a business putting Twitter to good use. They have a loyal group of followers who will get real-time location and other information via Twitter.

Another example that I can think of is a recruiting agency. Here you are trying to reach people beyond a very specific locale. Many people will drive 50 miles for a job, but they won't drive that far for ice cream. Twitter is an effective way to add credibility to the business while engaging with potential recruits.

Would I use Twitter if I were a hair salon? Well, it depends on a couple of things. First, are you a trendy salon in a large city? If so, I would do everything I could to build my brand and I would be tweeting regularly. Would I do it if I was in a city of, say, 15,000 people. Probably not unless I had a very unique selling proposition and a lot of time on my hands.

I hope these examples help you identify when it is a good idea to use Twitter. If you have the time, by all means use Twitter regardless of your business or locale. But if you are in a smaller market, the time may not justify the return unless, again, you had a very unique selling proposition that truly warranted the effort.

Final thoughts

For local businesses, the abundance of free social media platforms is a both a blessing and a curse. Free social media platforms like facebook, YouTube, and Twitter (along with Instagram and Pinterest) have given local businesses the opportunity to market their products and services to more people than ever before at virtually no cost except for time.

That enormous reach and low cost is truly a blessing. The curse is the fact that there are so many platforms out there providing local business owners with free tools to reach more customers. How is that a curse? Local business owners need to be "practical" in their marketing efforts and strike a balance between not doing enough and spreading themselves too thin.

Pay-Per-Click (AdWords, Bing Ads)

The two 800 pound gorillas in the PPC market are Google AdWords and Bing ads. Okay, Google is the 800 pound gorilla and Bing is more like a 400 pound gorilla. There are others, but since these are the two biggest, this is where we will focus our time. Not to be too redundant, but your time has to be spent on where you will get the biggest return for your time and money - Google and Bing. This book will refer to Google's AdWords but <u>the concepts are similar for both</u>.

If you are like the majority of local businesses, your advertising budget is probably pretty small. That's why you are reading a book on practical marketing; you want the biggest bang for your buck. To do this you will need to be very careful with your ads and target your terms with a laser focus. Do this and you will be sure to get the most sales at the lowest cost.

Why Google AdWords?

- ✓ A business owner can reach people who are actively searching for their product or service.

- ✓ You have control over the area in which you choose to have your ad displayed (Geo-Targeting).

- ✓ A business only pays when their ad is clicked.

- ✓ A business has complete control over how much money is spent.

✓ You can stop and start your ads, change your ads, and remove ads in minutes. This means you can manage your ads effectively. You can kill the ones not converting, tweak underperforming ones, and up your spending on ones that are working well.

What's not to like, right? Well, for one, if you create ads that don't get clicks, you won't be doing your business any good. And worse, if you get a lot of clicks but no customers, you are throwing money away.

So... let's make sure that your campaigns are successful.

Getting started

Successful campaigns begin with research. Before you spend a penny, you need to do your due diligence. Smart business owners will spend quite a bit of time in this phase in order to maximize their investment in PPC advertising.

Keyword research is essential. You need to focus on specific keywords that your potentials customers will be typing into the search engines to find your products and services. The tools that Google make available to you will help a lot in this area - use them!

Next, look at the ads that show up when you type in the search terms that you feel people will be using to look for your products and services. Which ads appeal to you and what is it that makes them stand out?

Make them an offer that they can't refuse

When your ad is clicked and the "web searcher" is redirected to your website, what do they see? Do they land on your home page or have you created a landing page that is targeted around your ad?

At a minimum, make sure that your prospect is presented with a professional page that represents your business well. I would also suggest that you present your prospect with a compelling offer that they would have a hard time turning down.

Geo-Target!

If you are a hair salon in Lakeland Florida, it probably will do very little good to have your ad displaying in Winter Haven. Be sure to identify where your customers will likely be coming from and set your ad parameters accordingly. Google AdWords will let you segment by state, city, zip codes, and more.

Ad copy tips

If your ad copy is poorly written or doesn't relate to your landing page, your ad will be a failure. You really need to take the time to ensure that:

- ✓ Your ad copy is tied closely to the keywords for which your ad is being targeted. Always include the exact phrase in your ad copy.

- ✓ Your ad is unique. If your ad reads the same as every other ad being displayed, you're going to end up spending more money for fewer conversions. Provide an offer that is different from the rest or better benefits of your product or service. Anything that will make your ad stand out.

✓ Coordinate your ad with your landing page. Don't just send visitors to your home page. make sure that your landing page completes the selling process started by the ad.

✓ Capitalize the first letter of each word in the ad copy.

✓ Capitalize the words in your URL to make it easier to read and stand out.

✓ Include the price of whatever you are advertising. You want to be making the prospect a great offer, so tell them what a great deal they are getting. If you are more expensive than your competition for some reason, tell the prospect before they click your ad and you get charged.

Test, test, and test some more

I always suggest that when business owners are getting started with PPC, they should limit their campaign to about 5 - 7 very focused "buyer's keywords." This gives you experience and limits your initial campaign setup time and ongoing maintenance. As you get more experience, you can eliminate the ads that aren't getting clicks or conversions and build upon those that are working for your business.

For example, if "Lakeland hair salon" is one of your target terms and it is getting you the results you want, you might consider experimenting with variations of the term. You might test out "hair salon in Lakeland" etc.

AdWords has tools to help track clicks and conversions and you should always be asking where customers found out about your products and services.

You will also want to consistently test different headlines and offers in your ads in order to determine the best possible ad with the best possible ROI.

Bidding on your ads

Google will show you bid ranges as a guide for your ad based on the keywords your ad is targeting. They have a vested interest in getting as much per click as possible. You, on the other hand, want to pay as little as possible per click. That is the nature of the game. You will be bidding towards the lower end of the range in most cases.

However, there is an exception to this rule as part of a longer term strategy. If you want to be placed higher, you will need to bid high initially. This is counterintuitive to your motivation as a business owner, but your ad placement is determined by a number of factors. The two most important are bid amount and CTR (click through rate). If you want Google to show your ad high, it needs to get some clicks. By placing a higher bid in the beginning, your ad will be displayed early in the search results. After you have a established a high CTR, lower your bids to the lower end of the suggested range.

Effective use of negative keywords

One of the cool features of Google AdWords is the ability to input "negative keywords" to prevent your ad from being displayed when people type in those words as part of their search query. Google supplies reports showing the terms that caused your ad to be clicked, so your list of negative keywords can grow over time and improve your ROI.

As an example, if you are a plumber and you might have an ad that targets the broad match phrase "water heater repair." But maybe you don't service commercial facilities so you would use "commercial" as a negative keyword so that when users search for "commercial water heater repair" your ad will not be displayed and you won't get clicks for a service you do not offer.

Some businesses do not compete based on price, so you might use "cheap" and "discount" as negative keywords to improve your ROI.

Only use search campaigns

AdWords will display your ad next to search results as well as on the Google content network unless you specifically change the settings. DO IT! When you are starting out, stick to search results. When you become an AdWords ninja, feel free to test out the content network feature.

Only advertise when you are open to receive calls

AdWords has the ability to let business owners assign specific hours for displaying their ads. If you are open from 8am to 6pm, only show your ads during that time. If you are a plumber who doesn't do 24 hour emergency services, don't show your ads after your normal working hours. This will prevent you from getting clicks that you really do not want and wasting money. Think carefully about your business and your after-hours lifestyle and decide carefully what hours you want to receive calls.

Test out device targeting

Another nifty feature of AdWords is the ability to target specific device types - PCs, tablets, and mobile devices. In many cases you won't care what kind of device your prospects are using for their searches. But in some cases, it can significantly impact the conversion percentage.

As mentioned before, studies show that consumers searching for a product or service using a mobile device are more likely to be ready to purchase. For example, a person searching for a locksmith or tire repair on their mobile phone is very likely to be in immediate need of your services.

Another cool feature for ads targeting mobile devices is that Google lets business owners put a phone number in their ads which consumers can click and call your business.

Need more reasons to target mobile ads? How about the fact that mobile devices only display five ads - two on top and three on the sides. On PCs, Google will display 10 ads - three on the top and seven on the side. As you can see, it is more important to get prominent placement on mobile devices.

Conclusion

For most local businesses, PPC advertising represents an opportunity that should be seized. Most local business owners can benefit from PPC advertising if they spend the time to do the research, create a compelling ad with a great offer, and analyze results

You may make mistakes in the beginning, but don't let this stop you from learning and trying again. Just be sure that you are systematically adjusting your ads and measuring your results so that you can hit upon the right combination of ad and landing page that will convert your prospect into a customer.

Email marketing

There are two very important points that every business owner should keep in the forefront of their minds every day. First, it is easier to sell to existing customers than to acquire a new customer. Second, you need to be constantly engaging with your customers. That is why email marketing is such a powerful weapon in your marketing arsenal.

But, from the lack of implementation of email marketing programs, one would think that this is perhaps the most well kept secret in local business marketing. Too often small businesses will focus their marketing efforts on obtaining new customers and they will ignore their current ones. Let me say it again, it is MUCH easier to sell to your existing customers than for you to get new ones. Don't get me wrong, you absolutely should be targeting new customers. Keep the sales funnel going at full speed, but don't take your current customers for granted.

Local business owners often, mistakenly, think that they have customer engagement covered because they participate in various forms of social media. But as it turns out, consumers actually prefer email. A 2012 survey was performed by ExactTarget which shows that 66% of Americans have made a purchase resulting from a marketing email. This email marketing statistic is pretty impressive when compared to facebook at 20% (email is more than 3 times as effective) and 16% for text messaging (email is more than 4 times as effective). In terms of purely consumer preference for types of communication, email is the preferred channel. Email was chosen by 45% of respondents compared to 36% for text and 13% for all other social channels.

What is a local business owner to conclude from this? When you are developing your marketing strategy, email should certainly be at the top of your list. Email marketing is not only one of the most effective tools that business owners can use to market to consumers, it is also one of the most cost-effective tools at their disposal.

I am not advocating SPAM emails to thousands of random email addresses that have been scraped off the internet. That doesn't work and will only serve to destroy your credibility and possibly get you fined for violating the CAN-SPAM act.

Rather we are going to focus on building an email list of our customers. Now why would your customers sign up for your email list? Because you are offering them something of value. To build your list, offer a discount. After you have a list, offer great specials so that people look forward to receiving your email. Give your customers a special offer or run a contest. Your options are only limited by your imagination. Talk about what is happening in your business. But be engaging and fun, don't just try to sell them something.

Your email marketing advantage

Email marketing is a must use tool for small businesses for many reasons. Not only are email marketing efforts cost effective, but if you implement and execute them properly, they will help your business build brand awareness and increase customer loyalty. Email marketing, even when outsourced to a company such as mine, will only cost pennies per message. Compare this to the cost of direct mail and you will see what a bargain it actually can be for your business.

Direct mail with design, printing, and postage can cost well over $1 and up to $2 per message sent depending on the number of units sent and the size of the mail. Also, studies show that the response rates on email messages are quite good ranging anywhere from 5 to 35 percent depending upon your industry and the message format (nice HTML emails convert much better than plain text). Whereas the response rate for regular mail advertisements are a huge success when they get over 2 percent.

The benefits of email marketing

If you still are not convinced that email marketing is right for your business, you are not alone. While it is in use by literally thousands of companies all over the world, many companies don't understand how important it can be or they misunderstand just how easy it is to implement, or outsource.

Here are a few ways that email marketing can help your business be more successful:

> Let me reiterate the main point - it works! As mentioned above, email is a consumer's preferred channel for receiving communications from businesses as well as being 3 times more effective than facebook and 4 times more effective than text messaging.

> It's one of the most affordable and effective marketing tools available to small businesses. According to the Direct Marketing Association, businesses generated $40.56 in revenue for every $1 they invested. While being a blended average across a wide range of businesses, it is

clearly effective. Also, given that the cost is mere pennies per message and response rates are magnitudes higher than direct mail, it is an inexpensive way of marketing your products and services.

➢ Another powerful benefit is your ability to grow your customer relationship while building greater loyalty and trust. By sending out well written and engaging newsletters, you will be building a relationship with your customers that will let them get to know you and your business better. This in turn will build trust. And we know that when consumers trust you, they will buy from you. Your customer retention and loyalty will strengthen and grow as long as you continue your efforts.

➢ Businesses can build greater brand awareness. Every communication you send will build awareness of your business and brand. You will be keeping your business and products or services in the minds of your customers. When it comes time to buy a product or service, people tend to buy from people they know!

➢ It is convenient for your customers. Businesses can place links to products and services allowing convenient access to information for your customers. The easier it is for customers to get information, the more likely your customers will actually read the information. This, in turn, allows you to boost sales.

➢ Another very compelling advantage provided by email marketing is that it allows businesses to market in a format that is likely to be read and noticed. People ignore billboards, we know from experience that direct mail gets thrown away with hardly a glance, and the same holds true for newspaper ads. But send out a well designed and engaging email newsletter and people pay attention.

> One more benefit, which may not seem so obvious at first glance, is the power of word-of-mouth advertising that a business can receive. Nobody denies that the most powerful ad is the referral from someone that the customer knows and trusts. Your email marketing campaign can result in these referrals as your customers forward your compelling offers and informative information to their friends and family members.

> Finally, it is one of the easiest types of marketing to track results and calculate the return on your investment. When running a business, tracking what works and what doesn't is crucial to your success and profitability. Your email service provider, whether you hire someone or you do it yourself, can provide statistics which show open rates and the number of clicked links. But beyond that, if you put in a compelling offer with a code that the customer has to give you to receive the offer, you will know right away if your campaign is a success.

While facebook, Twitter, and other social media may be getting all the buzz these days (and they can be a valuable part of your marketing arsenal) do not ignore this proven marketing channel. With all these benefits and many more not listed, you should be seeing the value of a consistent and well-planned email marketing strategy. Don't let your business miss out on such a compelling tool for driving business growth!

Getting started

Getting started takes a little learning curve and time but is not too difficult for most business owners. You need to sign up with a service that was designed for this purpose. I use MailChimp and recommend it for businesses just starting out. Currently it is free (another of the free tools available to business owners) for up to a list size of 2000 people and no more than six email blasts a month. That may change in the future, so be sure to check them out thoroughly before signing up. But this is perfect for most local businesses. And if you grow past the 2000 member list size restriction, consider yourself lucky and be happy to start paying the small fee for your monthly/weekly email blasts!

You may wonder why you would need a service. Because it is easy, free, they have great email templates that will give your business the professional look you need, and they handle all of the subscribe/unsubscribe processing that is required to fully comply with the CAN-SPAM act.

Next you need to give people a way to sign up for the mailing list. This is as easy as adding a box on your website where people can input their email address. The service you choose, in my case MailChimp, will have a simple API that any web designer will be able to implement (don't let them charge more than a couple hundred dollars unless your website was built with very specific non-standard tools).

From there, the service will take care of everything. The user will get an email confirmation to "opt into" your mailing list. This double opt in is used to fully conform to the CAN-SPAM act. As soon as they click the confirmation, they are on your list.

You may now be wondering how you get people to join your email mailing list. Well, you have to ask. Personally, my clients have had great results offering a discount at the time customers are ready to pay for their service. If you are a restaurant or a hair salon, offer the customer 10% off their bill if they sign up. Most customers have a mobile phone and they can do it on the spot. I will make a flyer for them, buy a stand from an office supply store with the offer, and also place a QR code that customers can scan with their smart phone that will take them right to the signup page.

Don't have the time to manage the process?

You should be able to outsource this task at very affordable rates. I will give my current charges for this process as a guide.

Making the change to the website is on a case by case basis since every website is different. By the way, you don't HAVE to make a change to your website, though it is recommended. I often create landing pages for this purpose for customers without a website (but that is not you because you have read this book and you know better).

Setup $99: Creating the flyer that explains the promotion, getting the MailChimp account set up, and creating a landing page for businesses that do not have a website.

Monthly $99 - $199: I use a tiered billing method that provides a substantial discount for businesses that are in the early stages of building their list. It is $99 per month for a list size of 1 to 500, $149 a month for a list size of 501 to 1000, and $199 a month after the list exceeds 1000 subscribers.

The monthly service includes formatting a nice professional HTML email every week with the information and offers you want sent to your list.

Not every marketing consultant will discount this way, so be sure to check around!

Customer referral program

Word-of-mouth advertising is the most effective form of advertising that a business can ever have. But getting the word out is not quite as easy as it seems. You may have hundreds or thousands of customers but are they telling others about how great your products or services are? Sure when asked, "which dentist do you use?" or, "who does your hair" they will tell others about your business, but you want them to be a little bit more motivated.

A trap that many local business owners fall into is the belief that if you provide great service and products, your customers will be referring your business all the time with no effort on your part. Studies show that while word-of-mouth advertising does happen, it isn't happening as often as business owners think it does.

Businesses that are not actively seeking referrals are not getting their share of them. You have many customers that are ready and willing to give you referrals many times over, you just need to give them a reason.

You need to start thinking of a referral program as a systematic process for getting high quality new customers through their association with other people. You want your customers to be actively telling others about how great your products and services are plus incentivizing those people to come and give you a try. You want an army of evangelists out on the streets witnessing to the masses.

Accomplishing this involves implementing a well-designed customer referral program in your business. With a relatively small investment on your part, you can get a stream of brand new high quality customers in your doors.

Customer referral programs are amazingly effective because they aren't viewed as marketing. No one is trying to sell anything to anyone. People are being hit with marketing all the time and we have become very good at blocking sales pitches out.

This is the ultimate reason that referral programs are indeed so successful. Your business is getting referrals from credible third-party sources that have used your products and services and are believers in the benefits of doing business with you. If they weren't believers, they wouldn't keep coming back to you.

These are recommendations from a friend that has no ulterior motive but to help others out. The reward you offer won't be enough to make someone who doesn't believe in your business suddenly start telling the world about you. Plus as mentioned before, if they didn't believe in your business, they wouldn't be your customer.

People are many times over more likely to believe what a trusted friend is saying versus reading an ad or other forms of marketing.

Getting started

While a customer referral program is not difficult to implement in a business, many business owners tend to get caught up in the details and fail to see the big picture.

So, the first rule is that in order to be successful, you have to have a reason for your customers to want to tell their friends and family members about your business. Let's assume that your business does offer great service and fantastic products at a fair price. If you didn't, you wouldn't have any loyal customers to motivate to be your new sales team.

At the heart of your referral program is the burning question, "what's in it for them?" If you want your program to be successful, you need to reward the person who did the referral as well as the person who is being enticed into giving you a try.

This reward needs to be of significant value to both the person doing the referral as well as the person who is being referred. If either party fails to see the value, your program will fail. Offering $5 off a $100 product or service won't work. You need to give something that represents meaningful compensation for the value that is being received by your business.

For example, a beauty salon may offer 50% off any service to both the person being referred as well as the person doing the referral. Given that a woman's cut, style, and coloring could be $100 or more, that's meaningful.

"But I won't make any money that way!" Well, not on the initial service, but read the chapter on the lifetime value of a customer again. That one customer may spend over $1000 a year at a beauty salon, and with great service by the salon, that customer will be loyal for years. Isn't it worth $75 - $100 to get that customer?

That 50% discount for both parties is probably break even, or a very small loss. Business owners will often cringe at the thought of "working for free" to get new business. While nobody likes to give up potential profits, it is not "working for free" it is *investing your time and perhaps some money into growing your business*.

Every business is unique, so be creative with the rewards you plan to offer and make sure that you are offering significant perceived value or your program will never gain traction.

Many business owners worry that they will lose money due to a few opportunistic customers referring, shall we politely say, less than ideal new customers just to earn the referral reward. However numerous studies have been done on customer referral programs and they all conclude that the positives outweigh any such negatives.

In fact, studies clearly show that referred customers tend to spend more and have a longer retention rate than other customers. That is a double win for your business.

Keep it simple

With all of the background out of the way, the next thing to keep in mind is that your program has to be easy for both the person doing the referral as well as the person being referred.

In the beauty salon example, a customer is given referral cards on which they write their name on the back and give to a friend. It doesn't get any easier than that. This card has the 50% offer printed on it which enticed the prospect to give them a try.

When the referred customer comes in they give the card to the salon and the salon has the record of the referral for when the original customer comes to collect their reward. This is very simple for everyone involved - salon, customer, and referred customer.

Think it through carefully

The benefits are plentiful and just about any small business can benefit from a referral program. Just be sure to take the time to think your offer through to ensure that you are offering enough to entice the referral and not leaving room for exploitation. Studies show that your customers doing the referring are not likely to try to exploit your offer. But it is always wise to limit any possible impact before a problem exists.

Taking the salon example, if the offer was refer a friend and each person gets 50% off their service, well that might sound simple enough, right? But what if the person being referred gets a $10 service for a new coat of nail polish and the person who referred them comes in and wants a $200 hair treatment?

This could be a coincidence or it could be someone trying to game the system. Either way, be sure to put disclaimers on the rewards such as "Receive 50% off any single service when you refer a friend*" where the asterisk fine print reads, "Receive 50% off your service when the person you referred purchases a service of equal or greater value. Where the friend referred purchases a service of lesser value, you will receive 50% off the lesser amount." Now you are protected and both parties will typically coordinate their purchases to maximize each person's discount.

A bonus benefit

Also, this could be utilized as a great way to fill the dead time in your business. If Tuesdays are a slow day for you, limit redemption to Tuesdays. Now you are getting new customers when you are the least busy!

What are you waiting for? Get started today!

Where to go from here

According to a June 2014 BrightLocal study, the best return on your marketing investment, whether time or money, were the following marketing channels:

1. Organic search results

2. Google+ Local/ My Business

3. Direct Traffic (people who already know about your business).

4. Google AdWords

5. Email Marketing

6. Referrals

7. Bing/Yahoo Local

8. Mobile Marketing

9. facebook

10. Bing Ads

11. Display Advertising

12. Twitter

After years of working in this business, I could have made this same list from experience. This study was actually published after I finished this book. It was just so compelling that I felt it should be mentioned here so that you can see that the things I am suggesting are based on more than experience, but also confirmed by independent research.

Look closely and you will notice that almost every one of these items has a chapter devoted to that topic. This is no coincidence. All of the methods I have covered are well established channels that have proven to be effective. Please note that there are multiple chapters devoted to why every business should have a website and how to build your website for the best return on your investment Why? Because it is the #1 marketing channel in terms of return on investment.

Your action plan

1) Get your website in order. If you have a website, evaluate it for looks and rank and make sure it is mobile responsive. If you don't have a website, start calling web design companies and get a quote. The most important thing you can do is **take action today**. Do not put it off!

2) Create your YouTube account and get five videos uploaded. These will be used when you do the next steps.

3) Create your Google+/My Business, Bing, and Yahoo listings.

4) Start building the major citations for your business. Even a few a week will make a difference in your rankings and will significantly help over time.

5) Get started on facebook. While it has a lower ROI, it is easy to implement and get started.

6) Implement a newsletter. Start collecting customer email addresses and keep in touch with them.

7) Implement a customer referral program.

8) Give Google AdWords a try.

9) Give Bing ads a try.

10) Start using Twitter.

Do not let the number of items or the perceived enormity of it all prevent you from getting started. Set a schedule and do one thing every month and in a year, your business will be significantly better. If you have a budget, you can speed up the process by paying an expert to do some of these things for you.

Human nature, for most business owners is not to do anything. Keeping everything the same as it always has been is a heck of a lot easier than implementing a comprehensive marketing plan. But it is your business, don't you want to do more than just survive? Wouldn't you rather take action and actually start to thrive?

Why not step out of your comfort zone and let today be the start of making your business more profitable than it ever has been before!

About the author

Lonnie Rakestraw is an author, business consultant, and entrepreneur. Lonnie teaches local business owners how to take advantage of online and offline tools to implement practical marketing methods that will drive sales and grow their business.

Lonnie maintains two offices in Florida. One in Lakeland (LakelandWebDesigns.com) and one in Fort Lauderdale (BriteFutureMarketing.com). He has helped numerous local business owners across Florida and throughout the United States and even built a website completely in Japanese for a Tokyo based client.

Lonnie is sincere in his desire to help local business owners get online and start growing their presence and getting more customers.

If you would like to contact Lonnie for a consultation, call 954-790-9739 and he will be happy to make arrangements for a session. If you are ready to get started, readers of this book can take advantage of a special package to get your business online.

Readers of this book that want to get online and start getting their share of customers already know that they need a website and need to grow their online presence. Since you do not need multiple sales calls and are ready to get started, you can get a 50% discount on our local business foundation package.

Local Business Foundation Package ~~$4999~~ $2499:

- ✓ Consultation session.

- ✓ Logo.

- ✓ A mobile responsive website with up to 10 pages.

- ✓ YouTube channel creation, 5 videos, and channel cover art.

- ✓ Google+/My Business (with cover art), Bing, and Yahoo local listings created.

- ✓ 100 local citations.

- ✓ facebook cover art and help setting up your facebook local business page if necessary.

- ✓ Twitter account setup and cover art to match your facebook page for consistent branding.